TEAM AMERIKICK "Where's Sensei?"

Sharon Kennedy Tosten

Tara Tosten

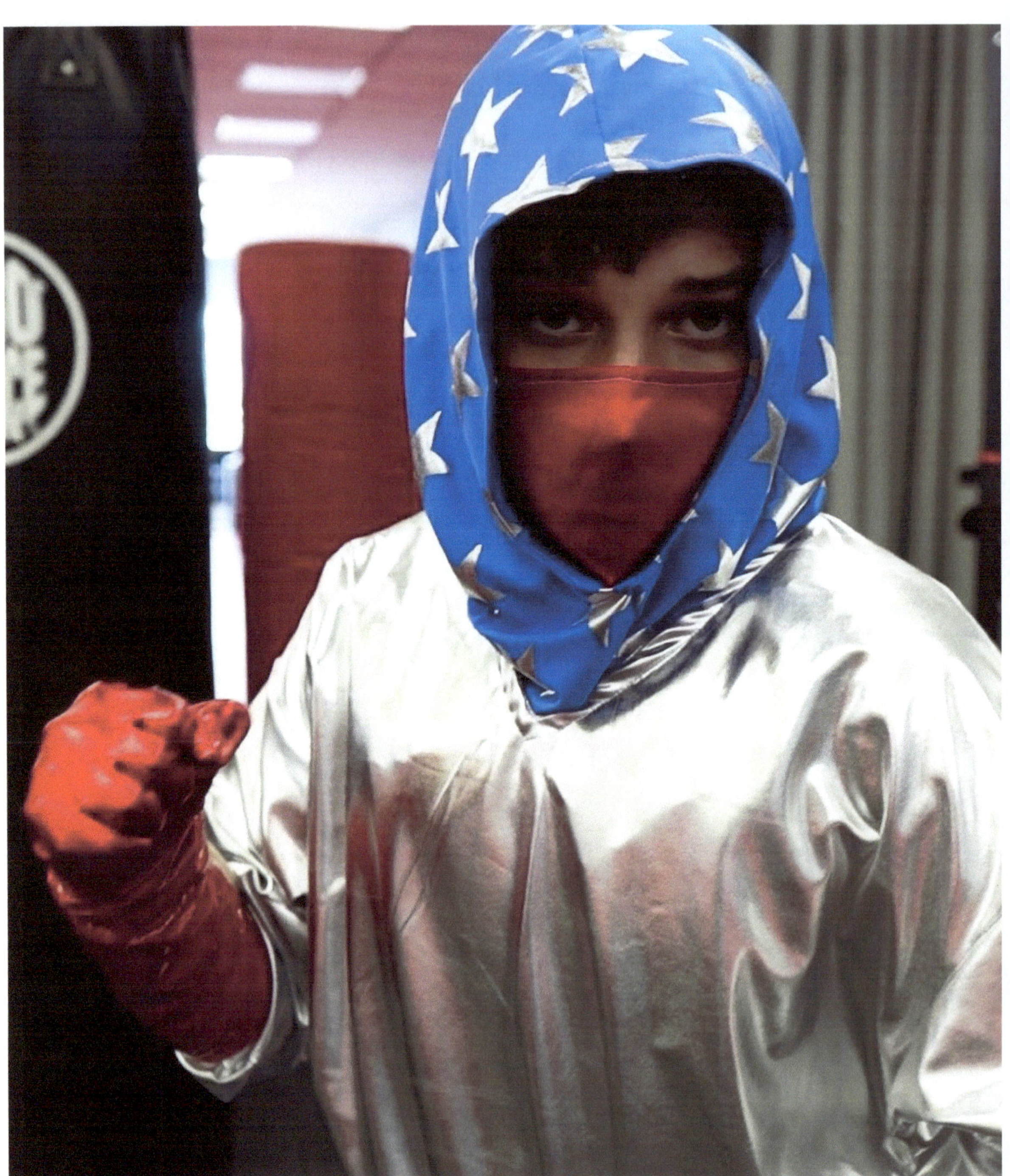

RJ, Rishi, Adam and Hai were excited to work-out. They got to the dojo and the door was open, but nobody was there. They looked around for Sensei Rob, but the building was empty. "Hey, no one is here?" exclaimed Adam.

"Where is everyone?" asked Rishi.

"Where is Sensei?" asked Hai.

R.J. noticed something on the mat. "Look, it's Sensei's belt! But where is Sensei?"

What they didn't know, was that the evil Narcissi, head of the Time Wasters, grabbed Sensei and with a "WHOOSH," and transported him back to the his dark headquarters.

Narcissi sent down his team of Time Wasters, Lazy, Screen Time, Boredom and Chillin' Out to destroy the dojo.

Meanwhile, Hai, Rishi, R.J. and Adam, all agreed to train hard until Sensei got back.

The Time Wasters were determined to recruit the Amerikick kids to their team. "We are in charge now!" yelled Boredom.

"I say it's time to surf the internet," said Screentime.

"Or do nothing," said Lazy.

"We just want you all to Chill out," said Chillin Out.

"NO WAY!" Yelled the boys, "TEAM AMERIKICK!"

Instantly they are transformed into TEAM AMERIKICK! *Perseverance* flashed in with a side kick!

Imagination spun in with a dynamic ridge hand!

Team and *Work* punched in ready for action!

The Time Wasters whipped out bo staffs and started their attack!

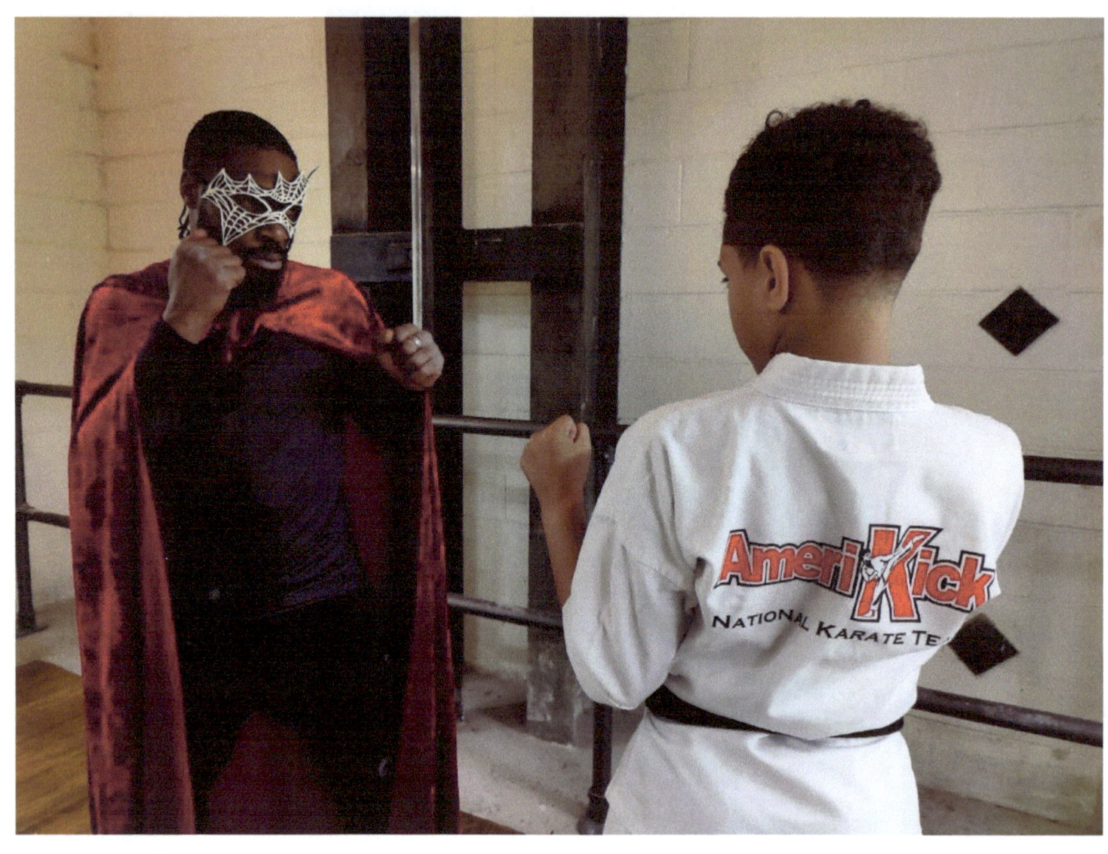

Meanwhile at Time Wasters Headquarters, Sensei Robert squared off against Narcissi.

The Time Wasters tried to SMASH from overhead!
With a loud CRACK the attack was blocked by Team
Amerikick!

Lazy took a big strike, but it was quashed by Team!

Work stopped a strong swing from Chillin Out.

Perseverance went hit for hit with Boredom!

The Time Wasters narrowly dodged a sweep to the legs.

But they couldn't dodge the power palm and were taken down!

While the Time Wasters wobbled from the effects of the power palm, Team Amerikick twisted the weapons away from their evil grip.

Back at Time Waster headquarters, Sensei Robert was finishing off Narcissi who was too busy looking at his SELFIES to focus on the battle.

Team Amerikick discarded the weapons and continued to try to find their Sensei, but the Time Wasters didn't stop! They went on the attack! Lazy flew at Perseverance with a butterfly kick. Percy dodged and went for a broom sweep as Lazy landed, narrowly missing him!

Percy leaped up for a spin hook kick, Lazy ducked as
Perseverance spun down-

smoothly whipping into a rear kick that pounded into
Lazy's belly and sent him flying across the floor!

Imagination was surviving an onslaught by Screentime with clever twists and turns!

The attacks ended when Imagination pumped out a thundering side kick, knocking Screentime SMACK into Lazy!

Team had some problems as Boredom cinched a headlock around the neck!

With a twist and an arm wrap Team reversed the hold
and had Boredom in a lock.

Boredom fought the hold, and Team put him down and held him to the floor.

Work was struggling, a leg sweep almost took him out-

--but he quickly rolled out and recovered.

Work ended the fight with a strong front kick, knocking down Chillin Out.

Team Amerikick forced all the Time Wasters into the center of the mat.

Team Amerikick grabbed some rope and they quickly bound up the bad guys.

With a final cheer, "Team Amerikick!"

\-   The Time Wasters disappeared, and Sensei Robert

appeared!

Now it was time to get back to training! Go Team Amerikick!